From EGG *to* BUTTERFLY

Written by David Drew

Photographs by Densey Clyne, Kathie Atkinson, John Cooke and Jim Frazier

Diagrams by Chantal Stewart

Collins Educational

An imprint of HarperCollins*Publishers*

From egg to caterpillar

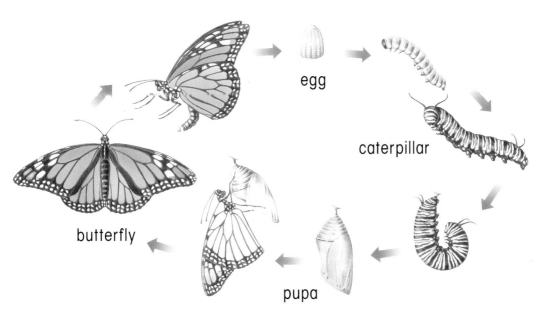

egg

caterpillar

pupa

butterfly

3

From caterpillar to pupa

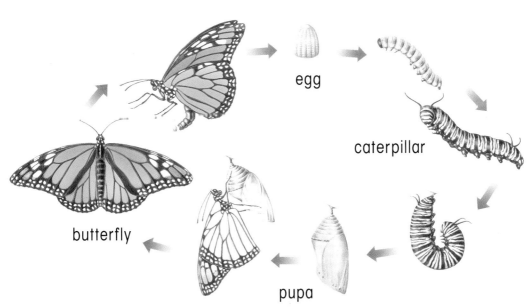

egg

caterpillar

pupa

butterfly

From pupa to butterfly

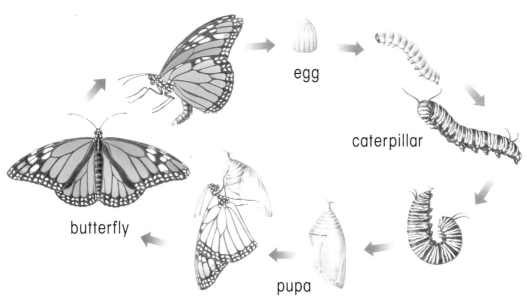

egg

caterpillar

pupa

butterfly

From butterfly to egg

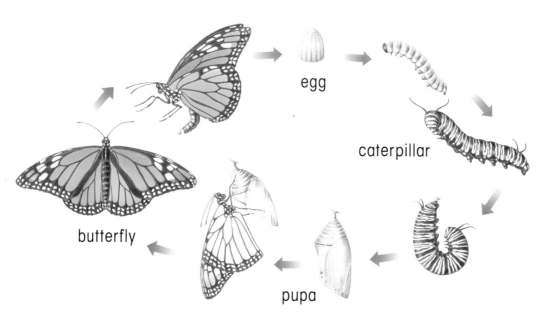

egg

caterpillar

pupa

butterfly